11/0ᴰ

Allergies, ASTHMA, and Exercise

by Celeste A. Peters

RSVP
RAINTREE
STECK-VAUGHN
PUBLISHERS
A Steck-Vaughn Company

Austin, Texas

www.steck-vaughn.com

Published by Raintree Steck-Vaughn, an imprint of Steck-Vaughn Company

Library of Congress Cataloging-in-Publication Data

Peters, Celeste A. (Celeste Andra). 1953–
    Allergies, asthma, and exercise /
  by Celeste Peters.
       p.   cm. — (Science [at] work)
  Includes bibliographical references and index.
  Summary: Explains what constitutes good health, how it can be maintained, and how diseases are treated.
  ISBN 0-7398-0140-6
  1. Health—Juvenile literature. 2. Medicine—Juvenile literature.
[1. Health. 2. Medicine.] I. Title. II. Series: Science [at] work (Austin Tex.)
RA776.5.P48   2000
610—dc21   99-27289
                                            CIP

Printed and bound in Canada
1 2 3 4 5 6 7 8 9 0   04 03 02 01 00

Project Coordinator
Rennay Craats
Content Validator
Lois Edwards
Design
Warren Clark
Copy Editors
Meaghan Craven
Ann Sullivan
Kathy DeVico
Layout and Illustration
Chantelle Sales
Warren Clark

Photograph Credits
Every reasonable effort has been made to trace ownership and to obtain permission to reprint copyright material. The publishers would be pleased to have any errors or omissions brought to their attention so that they may be corrected in subsequent printings.

Arthritis Society: page 32 left; **Dr. R. Chernesky:** page 37 bottom left; **Corel Corporation:** cover, pages 3 center, 4 top, 6, 7 bottom, 11 bottom, 12, 13 top, 14, 20 bottom, 21 top, 25 left, 28, 37 bottom right, 38, 40, 42 left, 43 right; **Rob Curle:** 24 left, 43 left; **Eyewire Incorporated:** cover, background pages 2–3, 44–48; pages 4 center, bottom; 5 top left, top right, bottom right; 7 top, 8 bottom left, 9 top, 10, 11 top, 15, 16, 17, 18 left, 21 bottom, 22 bottom, 34 top, 37 top, 42 right; **Franklin D. Roosevelt Library:** page 27 top right; **Kristen Higgins:** pages 3 bottom, 33; **Dennis Kunkel:** pages 3 top, 9 bottom, 23, 25 right; **Colleen McGinnis:** pages 8 bottom right, 34 bottom, 36 top; **Michael McPhee:** pages 20 top, 29, 31 top, 36, 41; **Publiphoto:** page 27 bottom; **Visuals Unlimited:** pages 5 bottom left, 8 top, 18 top, 19, 26, 27 top left, bottom; 30, 32 right, 39; **Linda Weigl:** page 13 bottom; **Stephen Wreakes:** 22 top, 24 right, 35.

Contents

Have you ever

wondered what it means to be healthy,

why you sometimes get sick,

or how doctors can treat certain ailments?

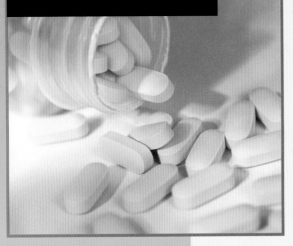

How you feel has a big impact on your life. It is easy to run laps around the school yard when you are feeling good. If you try doing the same thing when you have an upset stomach, you will not make it very far. The same holds true for taking tests. You need to be alert and healthy to do your best.

The human body has amazing ways to fight off disease and remain in top shape, but you must take care of it. What can you do to stay fit and healthy? What happens when you get sick? What treatments are available to help you return to good health?

FINDING LINKS

Society

If you know how diseases travel, you can avoid catching them. Many diseases are passed from person to person. From whom did you catch the last cold you had?

The Environment

Many things in our environment are harmful. Too much sunshine can cause skin or eye damage. Some chemicals cause cancer. Certain foods can trigger allergies and asthma.

Technology

Hospitals and clinics are equipped with powerful machines that help people heal. When properly used, these machines can help fight many different types of diseases. An X-ray machine shows a broken bone so that the doctor can set it to heal correctly.

Careers

Your mom or dad is probably the first person you turn to when you are sick. He or she can often tell what is wrong with you. Your family doctor also knows what to do to make you feel better. He or she can make a real diagnosis.

What Is Good Health?

"You're looking fit as a fiddle!"

How would you describe someone who is healthy? Is the person simply free of illness, or is there more to good health? The ancient Greeks believed that good health means having both a fit body and a fit mind. Your brain works better if your body is in good shape. Your body suffers fewer aches and pains if your mind is free of stress. Personal cleanliness, regular exercise, and nutritious food are also keys to good health. They help your body maintain something called homeostasis.

What is homeostasis?

In order for you to be healthy, the environment inside your body should always remain the same. The body's temperature must stay close to 98.6°F (37°C). The amount of blood and other fluids must not suddenly increase or decrease too much. It is important that chemicals are present in just the right amounts and that food turn into energy at just the right rate. Homeostasis is the process that keeps the environment inside your body the same when possible.

Imagine it is a freezing-cold day. You have been outside building a snowman for the past hour. Your hands, feet, and face are cold. Why? All your warm blood is flowing around important organs such as your heart and lungs. Homeostasis is at work protecting you. In addition, it might make your muscles twitch, or shiver. This creates the heat your body needs to stay at the right temperature.

Homeostasis also protects you if you go outside on a very hot day. It does not let your body get much warmer than 98.6°F. It cools you down by making you sweat. Sometimes homeostasis makes your temperature rise a bit higher. When you have a fever, the heat helps your body destroy the germs that are making you ill.

When you sweat, heat is taken from surrounding areas. This changes the liquid to gas, and it cools you off.

The body cannot always protect itself from cold. Hypothermia occurs when the body temperature drops below 96°F (35.5°C). These few degrees can cause serious injury and sometimes death.

BYTE-SIZED FACT

The body uses chemicals to control itself. For example, the mineral calcium can trigger muscles to shorten, or contract.

How does your body defend itself against germs?

Millions of germs try to invade your body every day. Germs are tiny organisms, such as **bacteria**, **viruses**, and **fungi**, that cause disease. You cannot see germs, but they are in the air you breathe and on the food you eat. How does your body keep germs out? What does it do when they get in?

Skin

Skin covers your entire body, protecting it from germs. The only way germs can get past your skin is through cuts, scratches, and openings such as your nose, mouth, eyes, and ears.

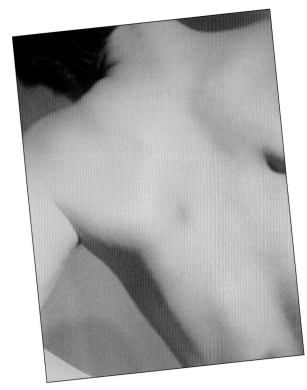

Mucus

Your nose and mouth are lined with mucus and tiny hairs called cilia. Mucus is a sticky, slimy substance that traps germs as they enter your body.

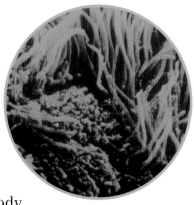

The cilia sweep the mucus and germs toward the front of your mouth so you can cough them out. If you swallow the germs, the acid in your stomach tries to kill them.

Tears and Wax

Tears wash germs out of your eyes. They also contain a chemical that kills bacteria. The wax in your ears is a trap for germs. It is sticky like mucus.

The Immune System

What happens if germs get past all the body's outer defenses? They meet up with its inner line of defense, called the **immune system**. White blood **cells** called phagocytes and lymphocytes are the immune system's most powerful weapons. Phagocytes flow through your blood and eat germs. Lymphocytes launch an army of chemicals. Each chemical, or **antibody**, attacks a different type of germ. It also covers the germ in a substance that attracts phagocytes. Chomp! The germ is gone. Your body remembers how to make the antibody for each type of germ it fights. If the same type of germ shows up again, the body fights it off easily. This protection from disease is called immunity.

Sneezing

Sneezing removes things that tickle the inside of your nose. Pepper, pollen, dust, and animal **dander**, the tiny scales shed by some animals, tickle. Some germs tickle, too. They do this by making the lining of your nose swell. A sneeze sends these invaders flying out of your nose at up to 100 miles per hour (160 kph)!

The smallest living thing is a virus. More than 25 million viruses can fit on the head of a pin.

BYTE-SIZED FACT

Who needs pain?

Believe it or not, you need pain! It can save your life. Imagine what it would be like if you did not sense pain. If you cut yourself, you could bleed to death without realizing you were hurt. If your clothes caught on fire, you might not know it until you were seriously burned.

Pain is your body's warning system. It sends a message loud and clear when something is wrong. Here is how it works:

When something damages your body, the cells in the injured area send out chemicals. These chemicals activate nearby **nerves**, the fibers that send messages between the brain and the rest of the body. These nerves send an urgent message to the brain. Almost instantly you feel pain in the injured area. At the same time, your brain sends a return message to the affected area that says, "Get out of there!" If the pain is caused by an outside force, such as heat from the burner on a stove, you immediately pull away from whatever is hurting you. Pain from inside your body, such as a stomach ache or a headache, can be a signal from your body that something is wrong.

Around 45 million Americans suffer from recurring headaches. Mental stress, diet, or a change in the weather can bring on a headache in many people.

The messages that go back and forth between an injured body part and the brain travel at up to 330 feet (100 m) per second.

BYTE-SIZED FACT

Can thoughts and feelings affect your health?

Have you ever worried about something so much that it made you sick to your stomach? When you do not feel well, do you watch television or read a book to take your mind off what ails you?

The mind and body are connected. This is particularly obvious when people are under a great deal of mental stress. Mental stress is the tense feeling you get when you take a test or perform in front of an audience. It feels like you have butterflies in your stomach. Mental stress can do many things to your body. It can make your muscles twitch and your heart beat faster. Sometimes mental stress can be a good thing, but too much mental stress over long periods of time can cause heart attacks, **depression**, and stomach **ulcers**, or sore spots and loss of tissue on the inside of the stomach.

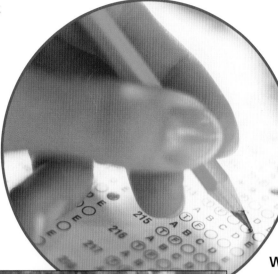

Worrying about an exam can make you feel sick. Worrying over long periods of time can cause many serious health problems.

People who are happy in life are healthier. Members of the International Center for Humor and Health visit hospitals to make patients laugh, and recover faster.

On the other hand, positive thoughts and feelings can have a good effect on your health. Happy people may be healthier and live longer than unhappy people. Love and friendship can be important, too. People who are surrounded by good friends, a loving family, and pets may be healthier than lonely people.

Preventing Illness

"An apple a day keeps the doctor away."

Good health is more valuable than a treasure chest full of jewels. You cannot enjoy wealth if you do not have your health. There are many things you can do to stay healthy. You can exercise regularly and eat nutritious food. You can try to get the right amount of sleep every night. You can deal with mental stress in positive ways. And you can avoid substances that harm your body, such as cigarette smoke and alcohol.

What does exercise do for you?

Are you a couch potato? No? Then exercise probably does a lot for you! Regular exercise improves your posture, lets you work off mental stress, and helps you sleep well at night. Best of all, regular exercise helps keep you fit. This is important because a fit body works best.

To keep in the best shape, you should exercise at least twenty minutes, three times each week. This keeps your heart strong and your muscles fit.

Several changes take place in your body when you exercise regularly. Your muscles and bones grow stronger. Your heart becomes a better pump. Your lungs work more efficiently, which means that they can deliver more oxygen to your body. Your body relies on oxygen to turn the food you eat into the energy your muscles run on.

Here is your challenge:

Your muscles need extra energy when you exercise. They need extra oxygen to make energy. How do your muscles get more oxygen?

1. **Take your pulse. Record how many times your heart beats in one minute. Also record how many times you breathe in during one minute.**

2. **Run in place or do some other fast exercise for two minutes.**

3. **Repeat step #1 right away.**

Do you see how your body transports more oxygen to its muscles? (Hint: Your blood picks up oxygen from the air as it passes through your lungs.)

Why are vitamins and minerals important?

Everyone knows that people starve to death if they do not eat. Did you know that you can eat plenty and still have poor health? What you eat is as important as how much you eat. The key to a healthy diet is eating a variety of foods. Food contains nutrients called vitamins and minerals. Vitamins and minerals do not supply any energy in food, but they are needed for your body to work properly.

Variety in your diet is important because not all foods contain the same vitamins and minerals. Imagine you ate nothing but oranges all day. You would get plenty of vitamin C but none of the mineral calcium. If you ate only fish, you would have lots of vitamin A but no vitamin C.

Certain vitamins and minerals are so important that you can become very sick if you do not eat enough of them. Before this was known, sailors at sea went for long periods without eating fresh fruits and vegetables. As a result, they often became sick and died from a disease called scurvy. Scurvy is caused by a lack of vitamin C.

Fruit is a great source of vitamins. It also contains a lot of sugar and gives us quick energy. But you cannot survive on fruit alone because it does not contain protein.

BYTE-SIZED FACT

Your body needs calcium to grow and maintain strong bones. The best sources of calcium are milk, cheese, yogurt, canned fish with bones, and dark green vegetables. So eat your spinach!

Should Children Be Vaccinated?

You probably received vaccinations at an early age. They protect you against catching dangerous diseases.

Vaccinations are usually given as an injection, and they contain a vaccine, or a small amount of dead or weakened viruses. This fools your immune system into making antibodies to fight the viruses. Your body remembers how to make these antibodies in a hurry if the same viruses strike again.

Before the invention of vaccines, many diseases crippled and killed thousands of people every year. These diseases are still around today, but the number of people who catch them is very small.

Most children are vaccinated before they start school. Some are not. Their parents do not want to take the risk. Vaccines are not completely safe. Thousands of people have serious reactions to vaccinations, and some even die. The numbers are probably higher because many cases are not even reported.

"The risk of catching a serious childhood disease is much greater than the risk of having a serious reaction to a vaccine."
New York Online Access to Health

"The dangers of childhood diseases are greatly exaggerated in order to scare parents into having their children vaccinated."
Independent investigator and writer on vaccines

"Unvaccinated children are not the only ones at risk. They might pass a disease to others who cannot be vaccinated." **Massachusetts Department of Public Health**

"There is no evidence that vaccines prevent diseases. There is a great wealth of evidence that they cause serious side effects."
Doctor who studies the medical literature on vaccinations

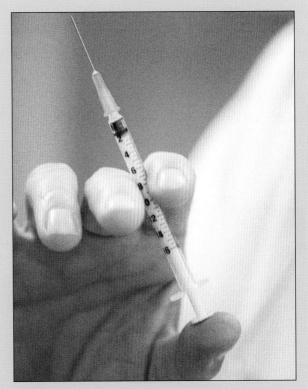

Which do you think is more dangerous, the risk of catching one of the diseases, or getting vaccinated? If you were a parent, would you have your child vaccinated against childhood diseases?

How does sleep help you stay healthy?

When you do not get enough sleep for several nights in a row, do you sometimes become sick? There is a good reason why this happens. Your immune system becomes more active while you sleep. It goes into high gear, fighting off germs that have invaded your body. If you do not sleep long enough, your immune system does not have a chance to do its job, so the germs may win the battle.

What is the right length of time to sleep? About 7 to 8 hours seems to be best for adults, but the amount varies. Children and young people need more sleep than adults. Newborn babies sleep an average of 16 to 18 hours per day. Teenagers need about 9 hours of sleep every night. Older adults need as much sleep as younger adults, but they tend to sleep less at night.

Elderly people are more likely to suffer from sleep disorders, such as insomnia. People with insomnia have trouble falling asleep or staying asleep.

BYTE-SIZED FACT

People dream every night, whether or not they remember their dreams. On average you have 1,825 dreams a year. That adds up to 136,875 dreams by the time you are 75 years old.

A warm room, big meal, and boredom do not really cause you to feel sleepy. You feel tired because your body is trying to tell you that you need sleep.

LINK TO Careers

Family Doctor

Do you like to solve puzzles? Can you stand the sight of blood? Do you enjoy helping people? Perhaps you should become a family doctor.

A family doctor is the first health care professional most people see when they have a medical problem. Sometimes the nature of the problem is obvious, such as a deep cut, a bad case of chicken pox, or a broken bone. Often it is a mystery. The doctor must talk to and examine the patient, looking for clues. Once the problem is identified, the doctor suggests the right treatment for the patient to get well.

Family doctors treat patients of all ages. They provide health care for babies, children, teens, adults, pregnant women, and elderly patients. Doctors spend many years learning how to do this. They go to medical school and train in clinics and hospitals. In this way, they gain experience treating many different ailments before they open their own doctor's office.

BYTE-SIZED FACT

Long ago people went to a barber, not a doctor, if they needed stitches or a broken bone set. Barbers also pulled teeth.

Many people stay with the same family doctor well into adulthood. The doctor gets to know the family's history, and this can help a doctor figure out what is wrong.

How is your hygiene?

Hygiene means staying healthy by being clean. Germs stay away from well-scrubbed, clean bodies. They live in places that are warm, dark, moist, or grubby. What happens when germs discover conditions they can live in on your body? Here are a few examples:

Body Odor

Did you know that sweat itself does not smell bad? Bacteria that make a home in sweat are the culprits. They create the smell we call body odor. You can keep these germs away by washing off after you sweat.

You should brush your teeth three times each day to fight plaque. Flossing your teeth is also important to get the plaque hiding in between teeth.

Strenuous exercise causes people to sweat. Body odor is easy to control with soap and a shower or bath.

Cavities & Bad Breath

Germs and bacteria are to blame for cavities and bad breath, too. These bacteria even have a special name—plaque. Plaque lives on the surface of your teeth. It eats the sugars left after you eat a snack or a meal. Plaque makes acid that eats holes right through tooth enamel. The acid causes cavities and bad breath. Brushing and flossing help to keep plaque under control. If plaque remains on your teeth, it can harden into tartar, which can only be removed by a dental hygienist, a person who assists a dentist.

Acne

Your skin makes a natural oil called sebum. Sometimes it produces too much sebum, especially when you are a teenager. The extra sebum mixes with sweat and dead skin cells, and forms an oily layer on your face, neck, or back. Sore, red pimples flare up when germs invade this oily layer. Washing with soap and warm water a few times a day helps to keep the oily layer from building up.

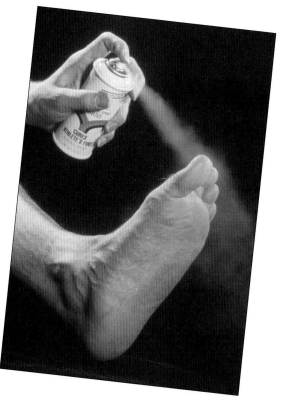

Athlete's foot is easy to treat. Often an antifungal cream or spray will clear it up.

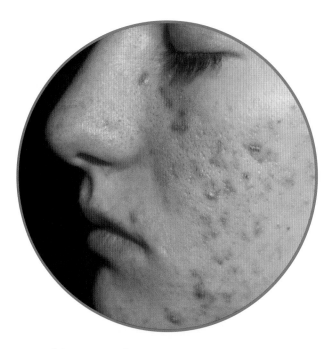

Washing your face is not always enough to stop acne. For extreme acne, there are medications that dry the skin and cause it to peel. The new skin is smooth.

Athlete's Foot

You do not have to be an athlete to get athlete's foot. Athlete's foot is an itchy condition that usually shows up between the toes. It is caused by a fungus that lives in moist places. The fungus hides in wet towels, sweaty socks, shoes, and showers. For this reason, it is a good idea not to share these items with other people. It is also a good idea to keep your feet clean and dry. Your shoes and socks should let air pass through them, so sweat does not build up. This will also keep away the germs that cause feet to smell bad.

What do cigarettes and alcohol do to your body?

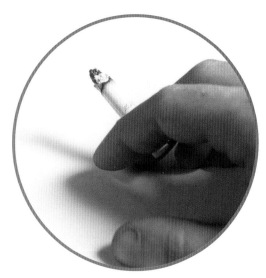

Cigarettes

Cigarette smoke contains 4,000 chemicals. Two hundred of these are known poisons. They can cause:

- bad breath
- loss of smell and taste
- face wrinkles at an early age
- stained teeth and fingers
- smoker's cough
- ulcers
- frequent colds
- emphysema (a lung disease)
- high blood pressure
- stroke
- heart disease
- cancer

Alcohol

Alcohol goes straight from the stomach into the bloodstream. Blood carries it to other parts of the body. When alcohol reaches the brain, it can affect how you think and how you act.

The liver is the organ that rids the body of alcohol. Heavy drinking over a long time can damage the liver and cause death. It can also cause:

- loss of memory
- loss of appetite
- stomach problems
- damage to the heart and nervous system
- skin problems
- dangerously low vitamin levels
- changes in behavior

BYTE-SIZED FACT

Once a person begins smoking, it is very hard to stop. Cigarettes can become an **addiction**, which means the body starts to depend on them. One out of every three young people who experiment with smoking is hooked by the age of 20.

Why Is Too Much Sunshine Dangerous?

Sunshine contains ultraviolet (UV) rays. You cannot see these rays, but they can do great harm to your body. They are especially dangerous if you spend a lot of time outside without UV protection.

Every time you get a sunburn, it damages your skin. The damage adds up over the years. It can cause wrinkles at an early age, and it can also cause skin cancer. More than 500,000 people in the United States develop skin cancer every year.

How can you protect yourself from the Sun's harmful rays? Wear clothing that covers as much skin as possible. Cover exposed skin with sunscreen that has an SPF (sun protection factor) of at least 30. Sunscreen is a chemical cream that prevents some of the UV rays from reaching your skin.

Your eyes need protection, too. Exposure to UV rays over many years can cloud the lenses in your eyes and make it difficult to see. This is called **cataracts**. Sometimes a great

deal of UV enters your eyes in a short period of time. This can cause temporary blindness. Snow blindness happens when a great deal of light reflects off snow into your eyes on a brilliantly sunny day.

Children should take special care with their eyes. The lenses in a child's eyes are clearer than the lenses in an adult's eyes, so they can be damaged more easily.

You can wear sunglasses that keep light out from all directions. The label should state that the lenses filter out 99 to 100 percent of UV rays.

Despite the risks of skin cancer, thousands of people continue to flock to beaches to get a suntan.

BYTE-SIZED FACT Dark sunglasses are not always better than light ones. What counts is the type of chemical that covers the lens. The chemical, not the dark color, blocks the UV rays.

Ailments

"You're burning up!"

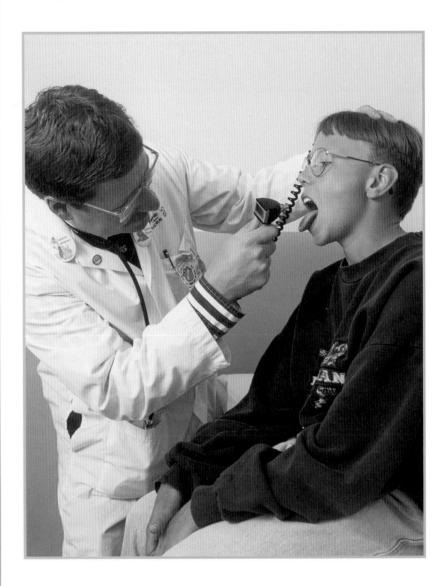

Your muscles ache. Uncontrollable coughing has awakened you several times during the night. Your nose is red and raw from blowing it. Sometimes your body loses its battle against germs, and you get sick. How do you know what ailment you have? Where did those horrible germs come from? Perhaps your body has developed a problem and refuses to work correctly. How do such things happen?

Cold, flu, or pneumonia?

You feel miserable. You have just blown through yet another box of facial tissues and you are burning up with fever. Should you go to the doctor? That depends on what you have. Colds, the flu, and viral pneumonia are all caused by viruses. Medicine cannot cure a viral infection. It can only ease the **symptoms**. What might help most is to get lots of rest while your immune system and the virus battle it out. Bacterial pneumonia is caused by bacteria. This disease is very serious. If you think you have it, you should definitely see the doctor. Bacterial pneumonia is treated with an antibiotic. (See page 36.) Only a doctor can prescribe this type of medicine.

> **BYTE-SIZED FACT**
>
> There are more than 100 different cold viruses. Your body develops immunity to one of them each time you catch a cold.

	Common Cold	Flu	Viral Pneumonia	Bacterial Pneumonia
Symptoms	• Sneezing • Runny nose • Sore throat • Dry cough • Fever under 101°F (38.4°C)	• Chills • Headache • Muscle aches • Fever over 101°F (38.4°C) • Fatigue	• Dry cough • Headache • Fever • Muscle pain • Fatigue	• Shaking chills • Stabbing chest pains when you breathe • Fever over 101°F (38.4°C) • Cough that brings up sputum, a mixture of saliva and mucus

How Does Disease Spread?

You have caught a cold. Who or what gave it to you in the first place? How do germs and viruses travel?

By Contact

People cover their mouth when they sneeze or cough. This leaves their hand covered in germs. The germs are left on anything the person touches. If the person shakes someone's hand, uses a salt shaker, or turns a doorknob, some of the germs rub off and are passed along. You do not know which objects you touch have germs on them. It is a good idea to wash your hands frequently to avoid getting sick.

By Air

Imagine you are in an elevator. Someone sneezes or coughs without covering his or her mouth. Millions of germs go flying out into the air—the very air you are breathing. How long can you hold your breath? Some people in Japan wear gauze masks when they are ill. This keeps germs from spreading. Surgeons wear a mask in the operating room so that germs in their breath will not infect their patients.

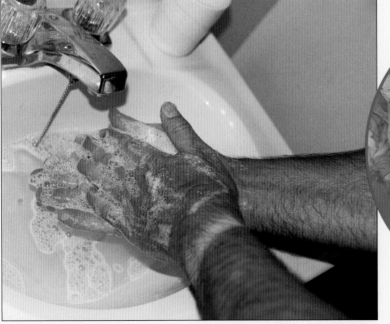

Rinsing your hands under warm water does not get rid of germs. Scrubbing your hands with an antibacterial soap is an effective way to fight germs.

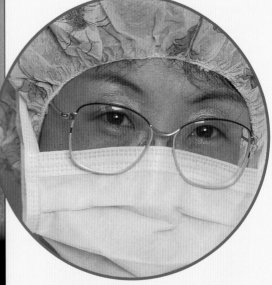

Surgical masks prevent almost all germs from getting through to the patients. The masks also protect surgeons from exposure to blood or fluids from their patients.

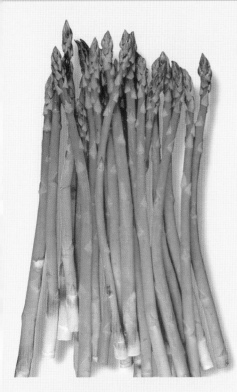

Vegetables should always be stored at regular refrigeration temperatures of around 41°F (5°C). This helps to prevent bacteria and illness.

By Shared Food or Water

Germs do not jump into a bus and go for a ride. But some germs do get into food and water. This gives them a free ride into your stomach. There are several ways you can protect yourself from these germs. Wash raw fruits and vegetables thoroughly before you eat them. Eat only well-cooked meat. Boil water before you use it if it comes from an untreated source. Most water in the United States and Canada is treated, which means that particles of dirt, harmful bacteria, and unpleasant tastes and smells have been removed.

By Insects

Have you ever heard of malaria or bubonic plague, the Black Death of the 1300s? These are two examples of diseases that are spread by insects. During the Middle Ages, fleas from infected rats spread bubonic plague all over Europe and killed millions of people. Malaria is spread by mosquitoes, most often in tropical countries.

Millions of people become ill and many millions die from malaria each year. Most of those who die are children under five years old.

BYTE-SIZED FACT Diseases that can be spread are called contagious diseases or communicable diseases. Sometimes an unusually large number of people in one community suddenly come down with the same disease. The outbreak is called an epidemic.

Have childhood diseases invaded your body?

Did you know that it is good to get chicken pox when you are young? It protects you from catching this childhood disease as an adult, when it can cause you more harm. Other childhood diseases are also dangerous and best avoided at any age. (To see how to avoid them, turn to page 15.)

(To see how to avoid them, turn to page 15.)

Chicken pox

Chicken pox has nothing to do with chickens. This virus begins as a rash that turns into clear, fluid-filled bumps. The bumps itch and form scabs. It is not good to scratch the bumps. Germs from your fingers can infect the bumps and leave scars. Chicken pox might give you a mild fever. It can also make you feel tired and cause you to lose your appetite.

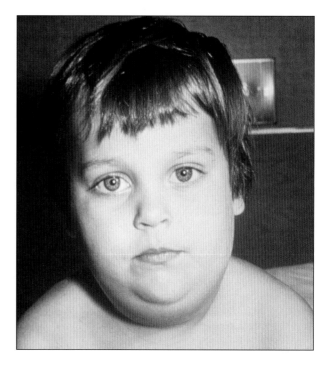

Symptoms of mumps appear between 10 and 18 days after the victim comes into contact with the virus. The swelling in the glands usually lasts for a week.

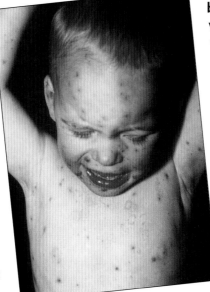

Children with chicken pox are very uncomfortable. It is often difficult to prevent young children from scratching their itchy pox.

Mumps

Mumps can begin with an earache, fever, fatigue, and loss of appetite. Soon the fever goes up. This is when the glands just below your ears swell. The swelling makes it painful to chew or swallow. Sometimes mumps leads to life-threatening diseases or rheumatoid arthritis. (See page 32.) Mumps can also prevent adult men from being able to father babies.

(See page 32.)

Measles

Small blue dots with red rings around them inside your mouth are a sure sign of rubeola, the severe form of measles. When the dots go away, your temperature rises and a red rash covers your body. Rubeola can cause pneumonia, deafness, or brain damage. It is much worse than rubella. Rubella is the mild form of measles that covers you in red spots.

Measles is spread easily from person to person. You usually get the disease only once.

Polio

Before a vaccine was invented in 1955, polio was a major killer and crippler of children. Some people who contracted polio did not even know they had it. They just felt as if they had a bad case of the flu. Sometimes the polio virus attacks the brain. It paralyzes the arms and legs and makes it difficult to breathe.

Franklin Roosevelt contracted polio in 1921. He did not allow his paralysis to stop him from being the president of the United States for 12 years.

Diphtheria

This disease begins with a sore throat, cough, and runny nose. If untreated, diphtheria causes a thick fluid to ooze from tissues at the back of the throat. This fluid eventually forms a membrane, or skin, that blocks the airway.

People can die from diphtheria because they cannot breathe. More people in Third World countries get this disease because they do not have access to medications.

What Causes Allergies and Asthma?

Millions of people in North America have allergies. This means their immune system overreacts to substances that are usually harmless, such as dust or certain foods. These substances are called allergens.

Allergies are caused when the immune system mistakes something harmless, such as a peanut, for an invader. It tries to destroy it by creating chemicals that signal a battle is about to begin. As a side effect, the chemicals also trigger allergy symptoms.

The allergy symptoms you experience depend on where the chemicals are released in your body. When they are released in the stomach, they

Everyday items can be deadly to some people. Animals, dust, grass, and peanuts are examples of things to which people are commonly allergic.

cause the diarrhea and vomiting associated with food allergies. When they are released in the nose and eyes, they cause the sneezing, runny nose, and itchy eyes of hay fever. When they are released in the skin, they cause swelling, redness, and hives. When they are released in the lungs, they cause swelling inside the breathing tubes. They also create a good deal of mucus. This can trigger an asthma attack.

People with asthma are often allergic to pollen, animal dander, dust mites, molds, or certain foods. Allergens are not the only triggers. Exercise, smoke, cold air, perfume, aspirin, and food additives can also cause an asthma attack.

What happens in an asthma attack? The breathing tubes leading to the lungs "twitch" and narrow. This makes it very difficult to breathe.

BYTE-SIZED FACT More than half of the people who have asthma are between the ages of 2 and 17.

Are eating disorders dangerous?

Did you know that you can diet yourself to death? People with eating disorders, or severe disturbances in their eating habits, sometimes do.

Most people with eating disorders are female. No matter how thin they are, they want to be thinner. People with the eating disorder anorexia nervosa actually fear being fat. They eat very little, and they exercise a great deal to work off the food they do eat. People with the eating disorder bulimia nervosa do not starve themselves. Instead they eat huge amounts, and then they make themselves vomit when no one is looking.

This over-dieting does several things to the body. It makes nails, hair, and bones brittle. It stops **menstruation**, the monthly flow of blood from the lining of the uterus. It also leads to other problems, including depression, worrying, and substance abuse. Most importantly, it damages vital organs, such as the heart, kidneys, and brain. You cannot catch an eating disorder, but you may inherit one. Eating disorders seem to run in families. You may also develop an eating disorder if you place too much importance on your looks. Models, ballerinas, gymnasts, and ice skaters may be at increased risk. They often feel they must be thin to please others.

Serious gymnasts are encouraged to be small. Some develop eating disorders to maintain their size, and some even take drugs that interfere with normal growth in order to stay tiny.

BYTE-SIZED FACT
Anorexia nervosa can start as early as age 7. Most people who develop this eating disorder do so between ages 11 and 14.

What is cancer?

Cancer is a disease that affects the cells of the body. A human begins as a single cell, the basic building block of all living material. This cell grows and splits into two separate cells. These cells divide and become four cells, then eight cells, then sixteen cells, and so on. This rapid multiplication continues until you have the trillions of cells that make up an adult body. Then the process slows down. The cells of an adult normally divide only when new cells are needed to replace old ones.

Sometimes a cell grows and multiplies out of control. All the extra cells it creates clump together in a lump called a tumor. If cells break away from the tumor, they can spread to other places in the body and start more tumors. When this happens, a person is said to have cancer. Unless the spread of tumors is stopped, these lumps begin to interfere with the proper working of other tissue and organs in the body.

One form of cancer, called leukemia, does not usually form tumors. These cancer cells involve blood and blood-forming organs in the body, such as bone marrow. They move through tissue in the body and can group together.

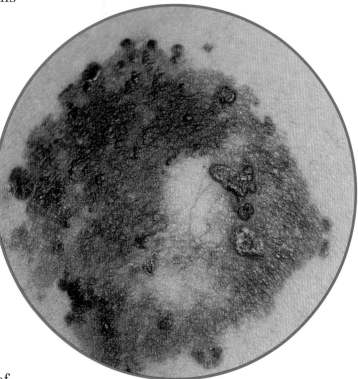

Skin cancer is a common cancer for women, men, and even children. Reports of new cases are increasing faster than for any other type of cancer.

BYTE-SIZED FACT

Not all tumors cause cancer. Tumors that do not spread to other parts of the body are called benign tumors. These are rarely life-threatening.

How does heart disease develop?

Do you eat potato chips regularly? How about hamburgers, deep-fried chicken, french fries, onion rings, or ice cream? These foods might appeal to your taste buds, but they could be harming your heart. Heart disease is a condition in the heart that prevents it from working properly.

Eating pizza or other greasy food once in a while is not harmful. But eating too much high-fat food can lead to heart disease and obesity.

Your heart is a special type of muscle. It pumps blood to muscles and organs throughout your body. The blood leaves the heart through tubes called arteries. Coronary arteries bring blood to the heart muscle itself. If something blocks a coronary artery, the heart muscle does not receive the oxygen-rich blood it needs to work. The result is a heart attack. If something blocks an artery leading to the brain, the result is a stroke.

What blocks arteries? Plaque is the main culprit. This is not the same plaque that builds up on your teeth. This plaque is quite different. It is a fatty substance that builds up on the inside of arteries. As it builds up, it leaves less and less room for blood to flow through.

There are two things you can do to help prevent the buildup of plaque—exercise, and limit the amount of saturated fats you eat. Saturated fats are found in foods such as red meat, poultry, dairy products, deep-fried foods, coconut oil, and palm oil.

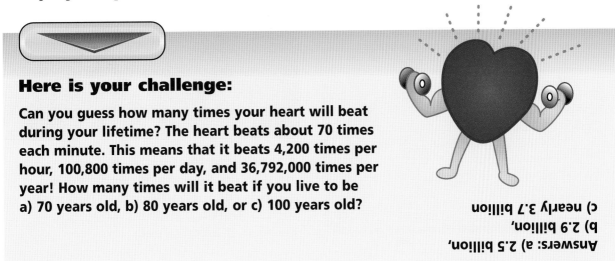

Here is your challenge:

Can you guess how many times your heart will beat during your lifetime? The heart beats about 70 times each minute. This means that it beats 4,200 times per hour, 100,800 times per day, and 36,792,000 times per year! How many times will it beat if you live to be a) 70 years old, b) 80 years old, or c) 100 years old?

Answers: a) 2.5 billion, b) 2.9 billion, c) nearly 3.7 billion

Can your body attack itself?

Sometimes the body's immune system makes a huge mistake. It begins attacking perfectly good body tissue. No one knows why it does this. The immune system simply considers this tissue an invader. This results in **autoimmune** diseases.

Rheumatoid arthritis is the most common autoimmune disease. It begins some time between childhood and middle age. The immune system suddenly begins attacking body tissue in joints. It sends out large numbers of white blood cells to do battle in fingers, toes, knees, shoulders, elbows, the spine, and other joints. This causes swelling and pain and slowly destroys the joints.

There are several other autoimmune diseases. Lupus attacks tissues in the skin, blood vessels, heart, and kidneys. Multiple sclerosis attacks the nerves. Some scientists now believe that Type I diabetes is caused by an autoimmune disease that attacks **insulin**-making cells in the pancreas. (See page 33.)

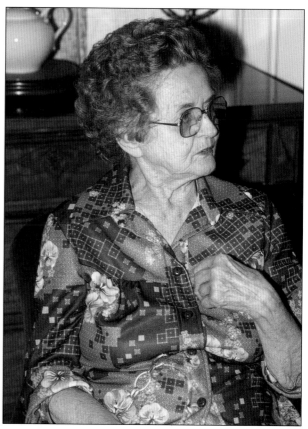

Arthritis interferes with what people want to do. Sometimes people with arthritis cannot participate in hobbies such as walking, knitting, or writing because of arthritis pain.

BYTE-SIZED FACT

Some people with arthritis can tell when wet weather is on the way. Their joints ache more.

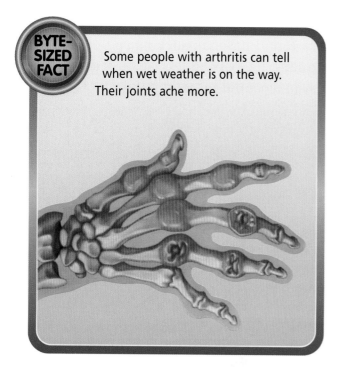

Why do some people need injections of medicine every day?

Some people with diabetes face the challenge of giving themselves an injection of medicine every day to stay healthy. They must have daily shots of insulin.

Insulin is a chemical that helps sugar enter the cells of your body. Cells need sugar because it provides the energy that they need to work. Without insulin to help process sugar, cells starve, and sugar builds up in the blood.

Where does insulin come from? An organ called the pancreas produces it. Some people have a pancreas that cannot make enough insulin. They have a disease called Type I diabetes. They must take daily insulin shots and follow a special diet.

Not all diabetics take injections of insulin. Most diabetics have Type II diabetes, and their pancreas creates enough insulin. Unfortunately, their body is unable to make the insulin work as it should. These people can usually treat diabetes with exercise and a special diet. A few must also take insulin injections.

Why treat diabetes? Untreated diabetes can cause heart disease, stroke, kidney disease, blindness, nerve damage, and difficulty fighting off infections. It is also one of the top causes of death.

BYTE-SIZED FACT Nine out of 10 people with diabetes have Type II. This form of diabetes usually develops in overweight people who are over 40 years of age. Type I diabetes most often strikes children and young adults.

Diabetics carry insulin kits with them every day. The kits help diabetics measure their blood and show them when their blood sugar is not right. They can then take insulin to keep their levels normal.

Treatments

"Let's put a bandage on that cut."

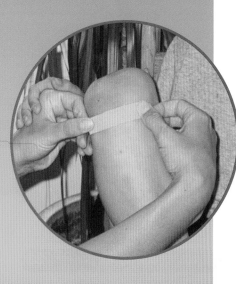

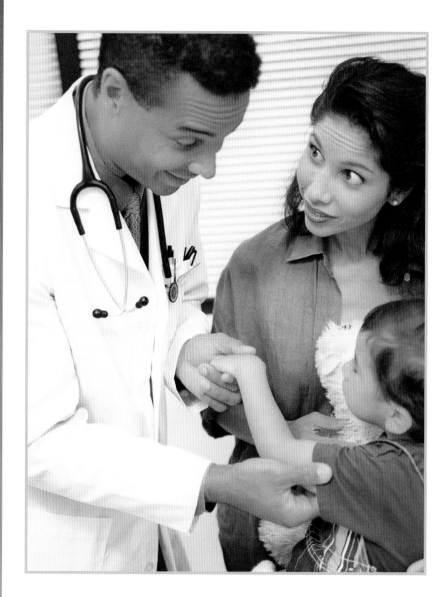

What do you do when you fall off your bike and scrape your knee? You wash off the wound and cover it with a bandage. When you have a bad cough, you take cough syrup. If you break your arm, the doctor resets the bones and applies a cast. And if your **appendix**, a small organ attached to your intestines, becomes infected, a surgeon operates and removes it. Is there some form of treatment for everything that ails you? How do pills, medicines, and operations work?

When is surgery needed?

Your big toe is really hurting you. It has for the last week. Is it time to operate? More to the point, would operating on your toe fix it? Or is there some other way to get rid of the pain?

Surgery, the performance of an operation by a doctor, is a powerful weapon against injuries that threaten the body, but it works only for certain problems. Surgery is used to:

- treat wounds

- remove diseased body tissue or organs

- rebuild damaged body parts

- ease symptoms, such as difficulty in breathing

- transplant tissue and organs

If your toe hurts because you stubbed it, surgery probably will not help. If it hurts because you have an ingrown toenail, surgery might be the only thing that will relieve the pain.

Sometimes surgery must be done immediately to save a patient. Serious wounds are stitched shut. Uncontrolled bleeding is stopped. Dangerous swelling is relieved. These are the types of surgery performed most often in hospital emergency rooms.

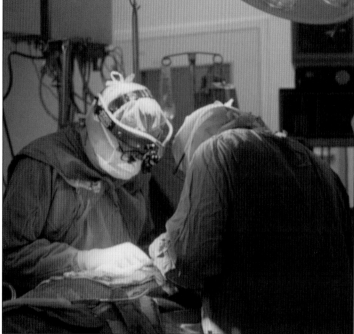

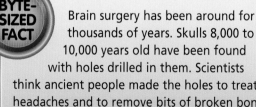

BYTE-SIZED FACT Brain surgery has been around for thousands of years. Skulls 8,000 to 10,000 years old have been found with holes drilled in them. Scientists think ancient people made the holes to treat headaches and to remove bits of broken bone after combat.

There are many different types of surgeons. Some focus on heart or brain problems, while others concentrate on cancer patients. Some surgeons perform general, non-threatening surgeries, and others treat the emergency patients at hospitals.

How do medicines work?

Sometimes medicines taste awful and are hard to swallow. What do they do inside your body to make you feel better?

Antibiotics

Your immune system is very good at fighting off germs. Sometimes it needs help. Antibiotics are medicines that weaken and kill bacteria. These germs cause infections such as earaches and strep throat, among other things. It is very important to finish all the antibiotics your doctor prescribes, even if you begin to feel better. If you stop taking it too soon, some bacteria will remain in your body. These will multiply and make you sick again.

Even with attempts to sweeten cough medicines, many taste terrible. But they help get us back on our feet and feel better.

Antibiotics kill bacteria, not viruses. They will not cure infections caused by viruses, such as colds, flu, and chicken pox.

BYTE-SIZED FACT

Antihistamines

You are having an allergic reaction. (See page 28.) A chemical called **histamine** is loose in your body. It is triggering your nose to run and your eyes to water. An antihistamine is a medicine that prevents the histamine from acting.

Antihistamines should only be taken when symptoms occur. If you take them every day you could build up a tolerance for them. Then they would not work anymore.

Painkillers

Analgesics are a type of painkiller. There are two types of analgesics. An anti-inflammatory analgesic, such as aspirin, dissolves in your stomach and enters the bloodstream. The bloodstream carries it to the place that hurts. Once there, the analgesic stops production of the chemical that signals the brain to sense pain. (See page 10.) An opioid analgesic, such as morphine, is much stronger. It goes straight to the **spinal cord** and brain to block pain messages. Stronger yet is the anesthetic used during surgery. It makes it very difficult for one nerve cell to send messages to the next, so pain signals never reach the brain. You black out.

Antacids

Your stomach uses acid to break down food and kill germs, but too much acid in the stomach is bad. It can contribute to the pain of **heartburn** and make ulcers worse. Antacids are chemicals that combine with acids and take away their power to do harm.

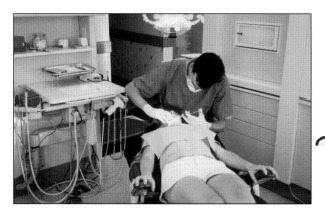

Dentists often use mild anesthetics so their patients will not feel the pain but are still awake. Doctors use similar painkillers before setting bones or stitching up cuts.

Peppers and other spicy foods cause heartburn in some people. But creams made from some types of peppers are thought to help ease arthritic pain.

What are herbal medicines?

Herbal medicines are medicines made from plants. You might find some of these plants in your kitchen or garden. Garlic, onions, marigolds, parsley, peppermint, raspberries, and rose hips can be used as herbal medicines.

Some of the first books ever written tell how to use plants as medicines. Early Egyptian, Greek, Indian, and Chinese doctors wrote about thousands of helpful plants. They used some to treat ailments and wounds. They used others as tonics, medicines that energize you, to keep people healthy. Today doctors prescribe many medicines. Nearly half of them include ingredients originally found in plants.

One popular herbal medicine is ginseng. The Chinese have used ginseng for thousands of years. Many people in North America now use it, too. According to folk wisdom,

ginseng can protect you from becoming sick. It is also supposed to make you feel more energetic. How? Scientists have discovered powerful chemicals in the leaves of the plant, but it is unclear how these work in the human body. Here is a mystery a future scientist might solve. Could that scientist be you?

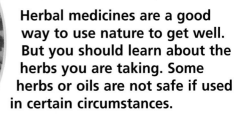

Herbal medicines are a good way to use nature to get well. But you should learn about the herbs you are taking. Some herbs or oils are not safe if used in certain circumstances.

Marigolds release an oil that repels worms that live on plant roots. This protects other plants around them from the worms as well. Marigolds are also used as herbal remedies.

BYTE-SIZED FACT

The National Cancer Institute has identified 3,000 plants that might be able to fight cancer. Roughly 2,100 of them grow in tropical rain forests. These forests are being destroyed by people and by pollution.

How Does Radiation Help Fight Cancer?

Many people who have cancer receive **radiation** therapy. Radiation therapy uses powerful, invisible energy called radiation to kill cancer cells. Radiation is more harmful to cells that are dividing rapidly. Since cancer cells are dividing more rapidly than healthy cells, they are more likely to be killed by radiation.

One type of radiation therapy uses a large machine called a linear accelerator. The patient lies very still in front of the machine. The linear accelerator then shoots a beam of radiation at the exact spot where the cancer is located.

What kind of radiation is used? That depends on where the cancer cells are located. If they are on the skin or just below it, the machine blasts the cancer cells with radiation that is not strong enough to go very far inside the body. To reach cancer located deeper inside the body, the accelerator shoots out a beam of powerful X rays, another kind of radiation.

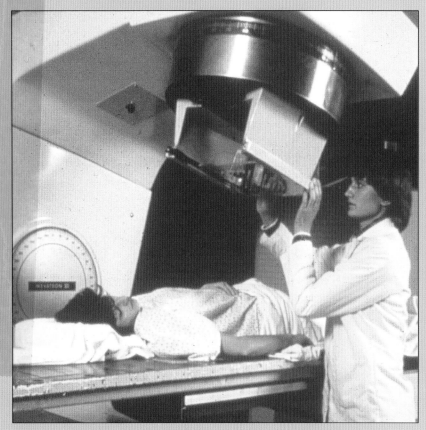

Half of all people with cancer choose to have radiation therapy. Many are cancer-free after their treatments. But the cancer may come back.

The linear accelerator is used to treat most radiation therapy patients. There is also another way to fight cancer. A container of **radioactive** material, material that gives off radiation, is placed inside the tumor or next to the cancer cells. The radiation it gives off kills nearby cancer cells.

BYTE-SIZED FACT

The X rays, or radiation, given off by a cancer-fighting machine called a linear accelerator are very powerful. The walls around the machine must be made of concrete 5 feet (1.5 m) thick. This protects other people in the hospital from being radiated.

Science Survey

You see adults smoke cigarettes on television and in the movies. You see them smoke in malls and at the park. You might even see them smoke in your own home. Do most adults smoke cigarettes? Is it OK to smoke? Researchers at the University of South Florida College of Public Health surveyed 813 fifth-grade students about smoking. Do you agree with their answers?

What are your answers?

1. Are you a smoker, or have you ever tried smoking a cigarette?

2. Have most people your age tried cigarettes?

3. Will it be OK to smoke cigarettes when you are in high school?

4. Is there a relationship between teenage smoking, drinking, and drug abuse?

5. Do most adults smoke cigarettes?

Survey Results

Of the 813 students who were surveyed, 53 were smokers, 85 had tried smoking, and 675 had never smoked. The smokers mistakenly thought that most people their age had tried smoking. They were also 11 times more likely than non-smokers to think that it would be OK to smoke in high school. Research shows that teenage smokers are more likely than non-smokers to drink and experiment with drugs. And what about adults? Nearly 3 out of every 4 students surveyed agreed that most adults smoke. Is this true?
(See the challenge below.)

Here is your challenge:

What percentage of adults smoke? In other words, in a group of 100 adults, how many of them smoke? You might be surprised.

Do your own survey. Ask all the people you know who are over 18 if they smoke. (Do not ask strangers.)

a) How many people smoke? _____

b) How many people do not smoke? _____

Divide the number of people who smoke by the total number of people surveyed. Multiply the answer by 100. This gives you a rough idea of the percentage of adults who smoke.

Answer: Less than 30 percent of people over age 18 smoke.

Fast Facts

1. Babies have about 300 bones. Adults have only 206. As you grow, some of your bones join together.

2. One of every three people sneezes at the sight of bright light. This trait is inherited from a parent.

3. The ancient Egyptians put moldy bread on wounds to help them heal. They were on the right track. The antibiotic penicillin is made from mold.

4. Today many people take aspirin to relieve pain. Early Native Americans chewed the bark of the willow tree. It contains the same chemical used to make aspirin.

5. Heart disease is the leading cause of death in North America.

6. Smoking kills more people each year than murders, fires, suicides, alcohol abuse, drug abuse, car crashes, and AIDS put together.

7. Teen smokers suffer from shortness of breath nearly three times more often than their non-smoking friends.

8. In healthy adults, 3 billion cells die every minute. There is no need for alarm. Living cells divide and replace most of the dead ones.

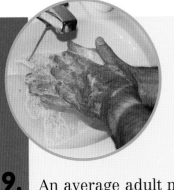

9. An average adult male has 10 to 12 pints (5 to 6 l) of blood flowing through his body. The average female has 8 to 10 pints (4 to 5 l).

10. Flu viruses do not cause stomach flu. Other viruses and bacteria are often at the root of vomiting and diarrhea.

11. Water alone cannot wash away oily dirt on your skin. Water and oil are made of tiny bits called molecules that do not stick to one another. Soap molecules stick to both water and oil molecules. Soap makes a connection between water and oil and washes them away.

12. The common housefly is a major cause of food poisoning. It picks up harmful bacteria on dead and decaying matter, and transfers it when it lands on your food.

13. People usually die if their body temperature rises above 109°F (43°C). A few survive. The highest body temperature on record is 115°F (46°C).

14. It is dangerous to exercise hard in very hot weather. If your body sweats away a great deal of water, you can become ill and collapse.

15. Sweat is mainly water, with a little salt and **urea**, a chemical found in urine. Millions of sweat glands cover your skin.

16. Viruses, not frogs, cause warts.

17. On average, women live longer than men.

18. There are five feelings that can prevent you from thinking clearly—hate, anger, hurt, fear, and romantic love.

19. Space sickness is much like motion sickness. Three out of four astronauts experience nausea, upset stomach, or dizziness in space.

20. Cigarettes can harm your health even if you do not smoke. Breathing in smoke from other people's cigarettes increases your risk of developing lung cancer.

Young Scientists@Work

Test your knowledge of health with these questions and activities. You can probably answer the questions using only this book, your own experiences, and your common sense.

FACT: Your body has many built-in defenses against germs.

TEST: Which of the following are defenses against germs?

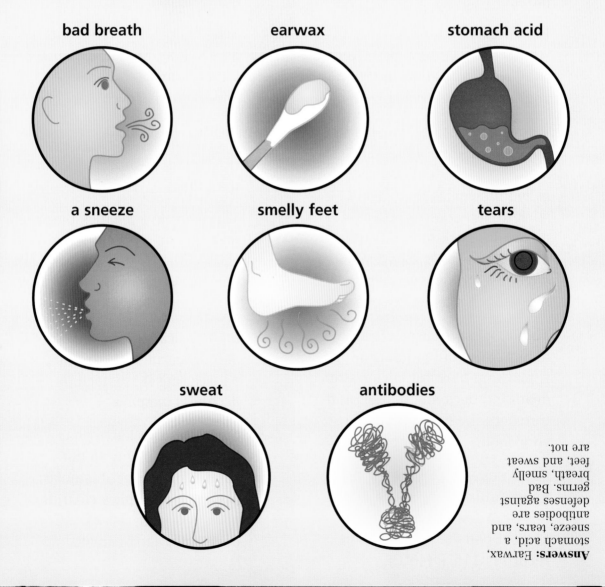

bad breath

earwax

stomach acid

a sneeze

smelly feet

tears

sweat

antibodies

Answers: Earwax, stomach acid, a sneeze, tears, and antibodies are defenses against germs. Bad breath, smelly feet, and sweat are not.

FACT: Your heart is made of a type of muscle that can work for longer periods of time than the other muscles in your body.

TEST: You will need a watch or clock with a second hand to do this experiment. Make a tight fist with your hand, then relax your hand. Repeat this tightening and relaxing movement 70 times per minute. This is how many times your heart beats every minute.

PREDICT: What will happen to the muscles in your hand after a while? Your heart does not become tired the way your hand does because it is made of a different type of muscle.

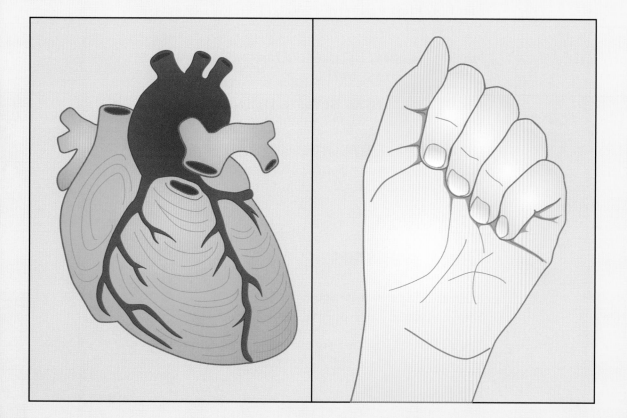

Research on Your Own

Health is a fascinating subject that deserves more investigation. The library, health care centers, and the Internet can provide information on health. Here are some great books and websites to get you started.

Great Books

DeStefano, Susan. *Focus on Medicines*. Frederick, Maryland: Twenty-First Century, 1991.

Gold, John Coopersmith, and Thomas J. Keating. *Cancer*. Parsippany, NJ: Crestwood House, 1997.

Landau, Elaine. *Allergies*. Ridgefield, CT: Twenty-First Century, 1995.

Markle, Sandra. *Outside and Inside You*. New York: Bradbury Press, 1991.

Suzuki, David (with Barbara Hehner). *Looking at the Body*. Toronto: Stoddart Publishing Co. Ltd., 1987.

Walker, Richard. *The Children's Atlas of the Human Body: Actual-Size Bones, Muscles, and Organs in Full Color*. Brookfield, CT: The Millbrook Press, 1994.

Great Websites

Kids Health Organization
www.kidshealth.org/index2.html

National Institute of Health Sciences Kids' Pages
www.niehs.nih.gov/kids/home.htm

Smoke-Free Kids
www.smokefree.gov/index.html

Glossary

addiction: Changes in the body that make it require certain substances

allergen: A substance that causes an allergic reaction

analgesic: A type of painkiller

antibody: A chemical made by the body to attack "non-self" materials, such as bacteria and viruses

appendix: A small organ attached to the intestines

autoimmune: Having immunity to tissue in one's own body

bacteria: One-celled organisms. Some bacteria make people sick.

cataract: A cloudy condition in the lens of the eye

cell: The basic building block of all living material

dander: Scales from skin, hair, or feathers of some animals

depression: A medical condition that causes a person to feel sad

fungi: The plural of fungus. Organisms that must obtain food from their surroundings but have no digestive system. They absorb "pre-digested" materials.

heartburn: A burning sensation in the stomach, usually caused by too much acid in the stomach

histamine: A chemical in the body that triggers allergic reactions

immune system: The network of cells and tissue that protects the body from harmful organisms

insulin: A hormone produced by the pancreas that helps sugar enter cells in the body

menstruation: Monthly flow of blood from the lining of the uterus

nerves: Bundles of fibers through which messages are sent between the brain and other parts of the body

radiation: High-energy particles or rays that can cause damage to living tissue

radioactive: Giving off high-energy particles or rays

spinal cord: The large bundle of nerves inside the spine

surgery: A medical procedure in which a living body is altered by removal of harmful tissue or correction of damaged or poorly formed body parts

symptoms: Changes in the body due to injury or disease

ulcers: Sore spots that are accompanied by a loss of tissue

urea: A chemical found in urine

virus: A simple organism that can multiply only inside living cells. Some viruses make people sick.

Index